T0370474

WHISPER
THE
WILD HORSE

CINDY SHANKS

AuthorHouse™
1663 Liberty Drive
Bloomington, IN 47403
www.authorhouse.com
Phone: 1 (800) 839-8640

Published by AuthorHouse 06/12/2015

ISBN: 978-1-5049-1709-4 (sc)
ISBN: 978-1-5049-1710-0 (e)

Library of Congress Control Number: 2015909322

Print information available on the last page.

Any people depicted in stock imagery provided by Thinkstock are models, and such images are being used for illustrative purposes only. Certain stock imagery © Thinkstock.

This book is printed on acid-free paper.

My name is Whisper and I was born under a large mesquite tree in the Tonto National Forest. My family was a small band of six wild horses, part of a large herd of over 100 that grazed along the Lower Salt River. We all roamed freely over the hills and valleys of the beautiful desert near Mesa, Arizona.

I was born at night to protect me from predators. My mom was still cleaning me when the sun came up. She licked me all over. It even tickled sometimes. I would try to move around but I was too close to a wire fence. I kept getting my head and legs tangled. Sometimes I would try to stand up, but the wires kept me pinned to the ground.

I would struggle and then get tired and fall back into the wires. I rested for a while and then tried once more to free myself. My legs were really long, 90% of their full size, but I was not very good at moving them. I was only a couple of hours old and not able to do very much, but I kept trying!

My mom's gray friend came over to help clean me and to show my mom what to do. I closed my eyes and rested a little. I was my mom's first foal and she needed a little help from her friend. Horse families bond together by licking and nuzzling the new foals.

Another mom came over to meet me, too. She tried to help me stand up and start walking, but I was still under the fence and having trouble moving. I wasn't afraid. I knew I was getting stronger and I would be walking and running soon. I liked having a family to help take care of me.

Finally, I was strong enough to scoot out from under the wires and move around so mom could finish my bath. I could feel my muscles getting stronger, and I just relaxed and enjoyed this rest time with my mom.

I knew mom was really tired when she lay down and closed her eyes. Wild horses don't sleep at night because of danger, so we take many short naps during the day. I was tired too, and I moved very close to her and rested. It was still early morning in the desert, and very quiet and peaceful. We both took a short nap, and enjoyed being together.

Later, when we opened our eyes, my dad had come to say hello. He is a gray horse with a black and gray mane and tail. He has white socks like mom. I love the way his mane divides over his eyes. He is a very strong and handsome dad. I know he will always protect us.

My mom's friends came back from grazing and tapped mom on the back to tell her it was time to get up. She needed to help me start walking and find milk. Mom nudged me to help me stand up. Our time of bonding and resting was over.

I moved around and away from mom and tried to stand, but it was really hard. I was between the tree and a fence, and I did not have a lot of room to move. I tried several times, but kept falling down. Finally, I was strong enough to stand on my own.

For the first time, I was able to walk and move around without help. I was still a little wobbly, but Mom stayed very close. I walked in circles around her and next to the fence. She would nudge me along if I stopped. I was so proud to be able to walk without falling! I felt clean and dry and strong.

I needed to find milk, but the first place I licked was mom's leg. There was something that tasted really good to me, and I knew this salty taste would always be my mom. Horses can taste and smell better than people. That is how we gather information about our world.

I was hungry. I finally found the special place on mom's body that had good, warm milk for me. My first taste made me feel very strong. Whenever I was hungry, or scared, or needed my mom, I would find my milk and feel loved and safe. I ate a little grass in just a few days, and I drank my mom's milk for almost six months.

Because I was now walking, the white horse thought I was ready to cross the road and head for the river. She took her foal across to the other side, but Dad immediately went after them. When he lowers his head to the ground, you know he wants you to move where he guides you. She and her foal turned around and ran back across the road very quickly.

Soon, I was steady enough to cross the road, and we all lined up to go through the V in the fence. I was the last in line, and I got scared and did not go through. I walked about 15 feet along the fence and was trapped on the wrong side! Dad and Mom did not know what to do.

Dad walked away and then Mom spotted someone across the road who might help us. There was a woman in a car, and she saw that we needed her. She drove down the road, parked her car, and came back to help us. She herded the other moms back to my side of the fence.

I tried to turn around and join them, but my head and two front legs were on the outside of the fence and my back legs were inside. Now what could she do to help me!

I whispered to my new friend by making a quiet, pleading sound. Mom and dad backed away and paced. They allowed the woman to come and try to lift me out of the fence. She put her arms around me and moved my head to the other side of the fence, but she could not move my legs.

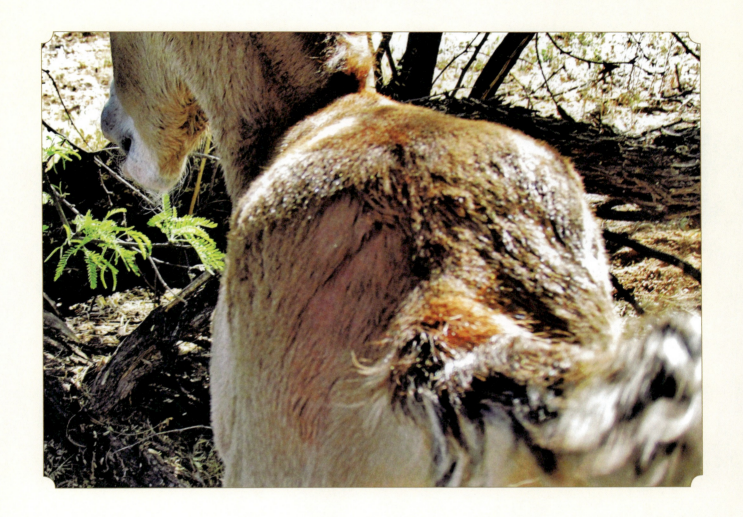

She finally lifted me completely up and over the fence and set me down in front of her. She guided me behind a bush to walk to mom and dad. All of the other horses went back through the V to the other side.

I joined mom and dad and crossed the road. I went through the V on the other side with no problems. My new friend followed us for a long time to make sure I was okay. I am so happy that she was on that road on that day to help me!

Mom and I went into the trees with the rest of the family, and headed to the river for our morning drink of water and rest time. It was a very busy and tiring morning, and I was just a few hours old.

Every day, my family and I grazed in the desert. We are wanderers and herbivores, and eat wherever we walk. We only eat grasses, leaves and some wildflowers. Since I was only a few weeks old, I still drank mom's milk and ate a few grasses. I played and sometimes nuzzled with a young colt in our family.

One day, when I was two weeks old, we were grazing along Coon Bluff Road when Mom and I saw my friend. We stopped to show her how much I had grown. My legs were almost as long as my mom's. I have white socks like mom and dad. My mom has a beautiful reddish brown coat and a black mane and tail. I hoped that someday I would be as beautiful as my mom.

Even in Arizona it gets cold in the winter. It is colder near the river than it is in the city. We have monsoon rains and sometimes there is even ice on the desert plants. But when the sun comes up, the ice melts quickly. My first winter, I grew a thick fuzzy coat, which helped me stay dry and warm through the whole season.

When winter was over, the wildflowers bloomed and the desert was beautiful. The days got warmer. To get rid of our heavy winter coats, we liked to roll around in the dirt and shed the hair. This also helped us with insects in the spring and summer. I just liked it because it felt good.

In the spring, when I turned a year old, I lost my fuzzy winter coat. Now, I was almost as tall as my mom and looked more like her. My new coat was a darker shade of reddish brown, and my mane and tail were dark black. My legs were long and strong and I had three white socks. I had grown up.

Now our family of six was only five. The other young horse was a colt, and when he got old enough, he had to leave the family and join the bachelor band. He will be looking for a mare so that he can start a family of his own. I think we will have new foals in our family before summer comes.

The bachelor band roams the desert looking for mares (females) to steal away from the other family bands. One of the bachelors will fight with a family's stallion (male) to win a mare. They may even fight to steal the whole band! These fights are loud and dangerous, often leaving terrible scars on both horses.

The bachelors have a lot of energy. They often run through the desert making a lot of noise and raising a lot of dust. They even practice fighting with each other. The rest of the family bands stay safely out of their way.

There were many days when we grazed along the river and on the bluffs above the water at Coon Bluff. In the summer, when it is warm, we stay closer to the coolness in the trees. At this time of year, the open desert with its many cacti is very hot, and does not have a lot of food for us.

When the spring wildflowers were gone, we ate dried grasses and leaves from the mesquite trees. We sometimes leaned against the trees to scratch, especially when the insects were biting. It always feels good just to scratch an itch. We grazed and ate about 16 hours a day. We had to keep moving and finding new food.

We went to the river to drink every day. It is the only place in the desert for us to find water. We need to drink more water in the summer because the desert becomes very hot – more than 100 degrees every day for weeks. We often cross the river to cool off and to graze on the other side.

There were often fights in the water between two stallions. They both would have a band of their own, but one of them would try to steal a mare from the other band. They often kick the water to show how strong they are. They do this for a short time and then turn and walk back to their own band.

One summer day when I was two years old, my family and I went to Coon Bluff to graze and drink at the river. Early in the morning, many of the bands were crossing the river and walking through the empty picnic area. They would go through a V in the fence to graze under the trees. My band followed the others through the V. We were in a straight line and I was near the end.

As I walked along the trail, I looked over and saw my friend. She had lifted me out of the wire fence when I was a foal, and I had never forgotten her. I left the line and walked over to see her. I knew she had helped me and was kind. I was happy to see her. She had tears in her eyes.

I started to walk closer to my friend, but dad looked over and saw me. He made a sound that told me to get back in line and stay with the family. I had to walk away from my friend, but she followed us into the trees where we stopped to graze. I walked up to her a few times, but she always moved behind a tree. I was very glad to see her, and let her know that I remembered her.

I have seen my friend many times these last three years. She was there one day when we were running through Coon Bluff and heading to the river. I was with the whole family and could not stop. But I know she was happy to see me, and I was happy to see her.

Now, I am almost three years old. I was very surprised to walk through the tall grass towards the river and see my friend on the other side watching me. I had a big surprise for her. I am a new mother! I have a foal named Wade, and he is beautiful. He was very curious about the woman across the river and watched her carefully.

Wade loves to be near the river. He grazes on the grass and wades in the water. He is always curious and sniffing everything. He loves to nuzzle and run and play. When we graze, my ears are usually relaxed. Wade's ears are always pointing in different directions because he is paying attention to every sound he hears. If they ever go straight back, I will know he is ready to fight.

Wade is the same color that I was when I was born. I wonder if he will be dark like me, or lighter like my mom. His mane is reddish and his tail is still very curly and mostly light brown.

He has very long legs, so I know he will be tall. I see a lot of white on his legs, so he will have socks like the rest of the family. He may have stockings that are longer and above the knee. Watching him grow will be so exciting!

Just like every baby, he has to take time from his play to have his milk and rest for a while. In a few months he will be weaned. Soon after that, he will leave this family, join the bachelor band, and learn to fight the other stallions for his own band of mares.

There were three bands of horses at the river that day. There were a lot of new foals this year and they all looked very healthy. One of the stallions tried to come to our band and steal a mare, but dad chased him away.

Dad moved us down the river so we could graze and rest alone. Dad rests standing up with his legs locked. That is how we all rest most of the time, so we can run quickly if there is danger. If we feel safe, we may lay down to rest for a short time. Most of the foals rest lying flat on the ground. Today we are all standing because of the other bands of horses.

A few days later, very early in the morning, my family was grazing near the highway. I did not want to take Wade close to the road, so we stayed behind the trees. When we moved out into the sand, he had some trouble eating and made a really funny face. Maybe he didn't like the grass and prefers milk.

When we joined the family to walk down the wash towards the river, Wade decided to go exploring in the bushes. I had to chase him and guide him back to the wash. Wade didn't really care. He is always playing and jumping around. I am so happy to be a mom. The Salt River Valley is a beautiful place to live and raise my family.

ACKNOWLEDGMENTS

The inspiration for this book comes directly from my love for the desert and the wild horses. For many years I have experienced profound peace and joy in my mornings at the Salt River. I hope this book introduces you to the beauty and energy of the desert. Thank you to all of my friends who have constantly encouraged me to share my words and pictures. A special thank you to Fred Tillman and Steve Taylor for their patience, hard work and expertise while editing my stories. You are the best! Thank you to Dustin Harling for making my scanning of pictures so much better, faster and easier. And thank you to my good friend, hiking buddy and fellow horse lover Kathy Leduc for sharing the back cover picture from one of our best days with the horses. Enjoy!